T0168591

A-MAZE-ING
PEANUTS®

100 MAZES FEATURING CHARLIE BROWN AND FRIENDS

CHARLES M. SCHULZ
JOE WOS

Andrews McMeel
PUBLISHING®

Andrews McMeel Publishing
a division of Andrews McMeel Universal
1130 Walnut Street, Kansas City, Missouri 64106

www.andrewsmcmeel.com

21 22 23 24 25 RLP 10 9 8 7 6 5 4 3 2 1

ISBN: 978-1-5248-6972-4

Made by:
Shenzhen Reliance Printing Co., Ltd
Address and location of manufacturer:
25 Longshan Industrial Zone, Nanling,
Longgang District, Shenzhen, China, 518114
1st printing—07/05/21

Editor: Kevin Kotur
Art Director: Holly Swayne
Production Editor: Margaret Daniels
Production Manager: Tamara Haus

ATTENTION: SCHOOLS AND BUSINESSES

LEVEL 1

LEVEL 1

LEVEL 1

LEVEL 1

LEVEL 1

LEVEL 1

LEVEL 1

LEVEL 1

LEVEL 1

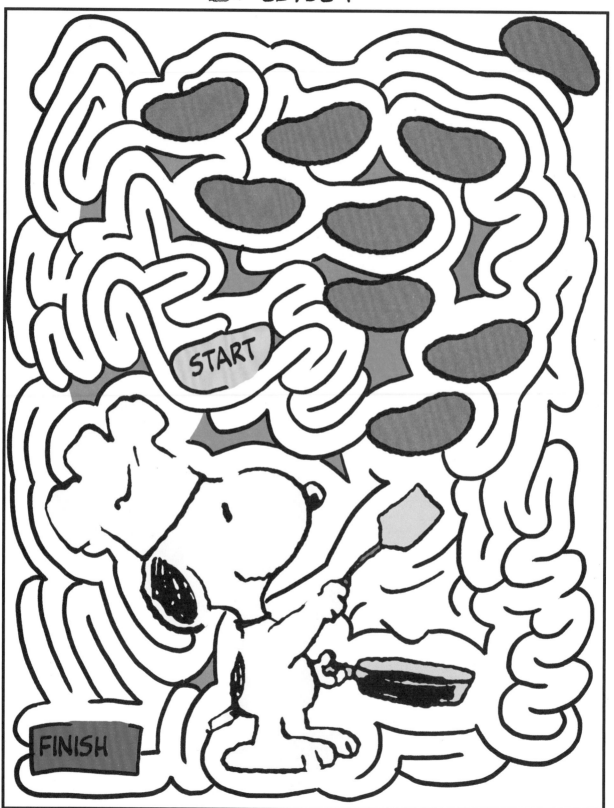

LEVEL 2

LEVEL 2

LEVEL 2

LEVEL 2

LEVEL 2

LEVEL 2

LEVEL 2

LEVEL 2

LEVEL 2

LEVEL 2

LEVEL 2

LEVEL 2

LEVEL 2

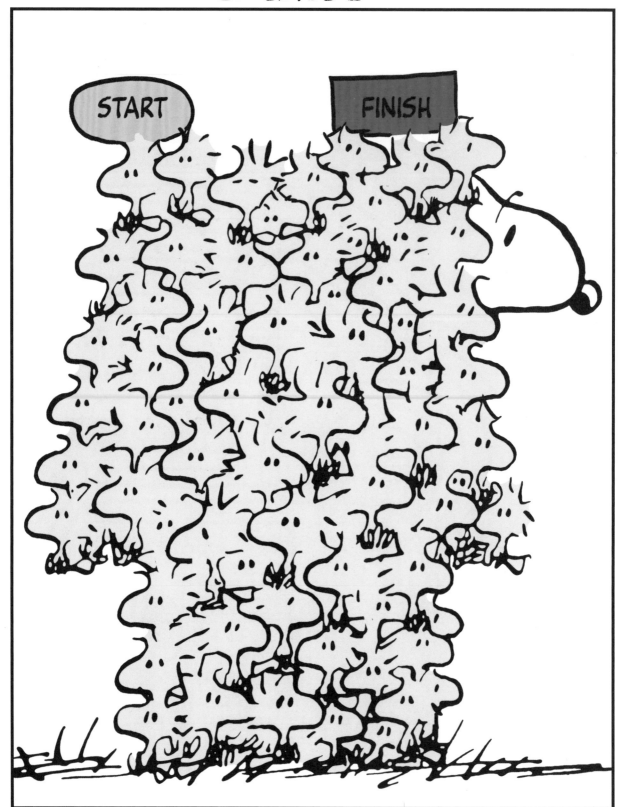

LEVEL 2

LEVEL 2

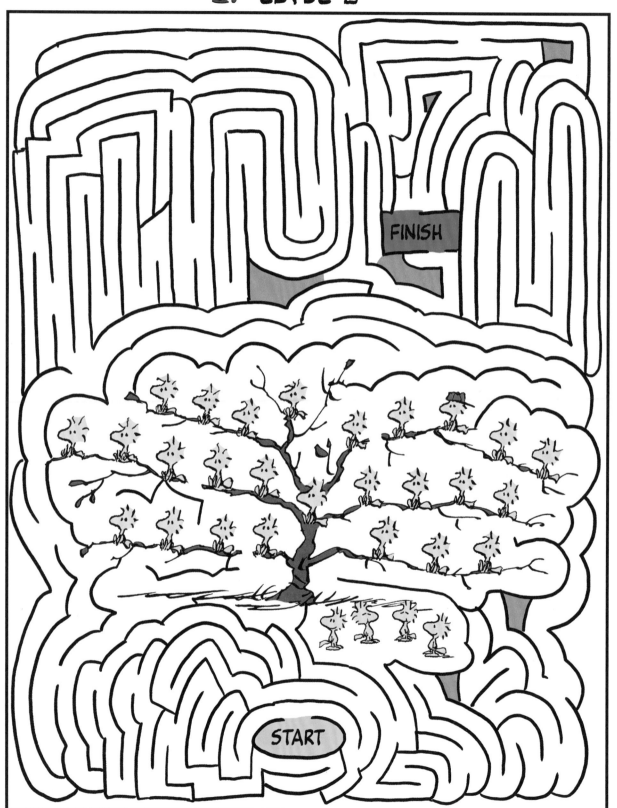

FINISH

START

LEVEL 3

LEVEL 3

LEVEL 3

LEVEL 3

LEVEL 3

LEVEL 3

LEVEL 3

LEVEL 3

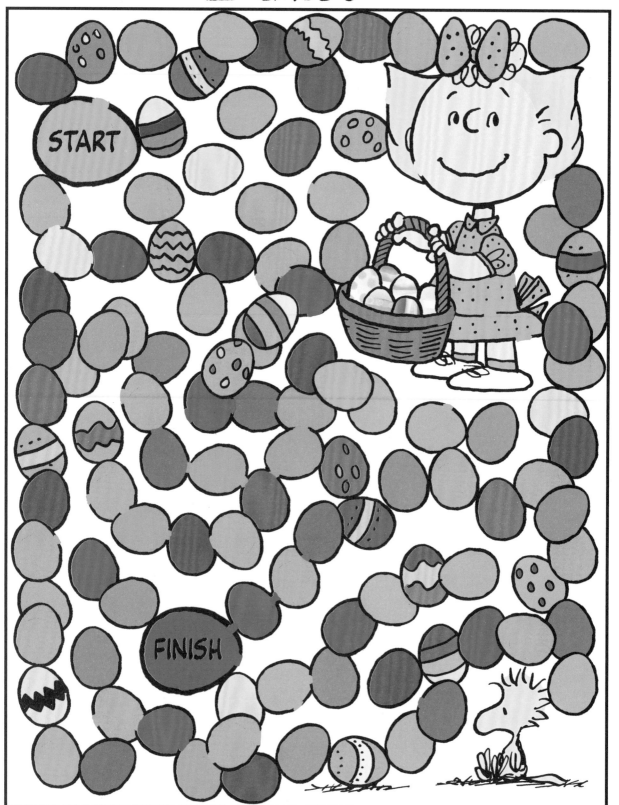

LEVEL 3

LEVEL 3

LEVEL 3

LEVEL 3

LEVEL 3

LEVEL 3

LEVEL 3

LEVEL 3

LEVEL 3

START

FINISH

LEVEL 3

LEVEL 3

LEVEL 3

 LEVEL 3

LEVEL 3

LEVEL 3

LEVEL 3

LEVEL 3

START

FINISH

LEVEL 3

LEVEL 3

START

FINISH

LEVEL 3

LEVEL 3

LEVEL 4

LEVEL 4

LEVEL 4

LEVEL 4

LEVEL 4

LEVEL 4

LEVEL 4

LEVEL 4

LEVEL 4

LEVEL 4

FINISH

START

LEVEL 4

LEVEL 4

START

FINISH

LEVEL 4

LEVEL 4

LEVEL 4

 **LEVEL 4**

START

FINISH

LEVEL 4

LEVEL 4

LEVEL 4

FINISH

JAM

START

 LEVEL 4

LEVEL 4

LEVEL 4

LEVEL 5

LEVEL 5

LEVEL 5

LEVEL 5

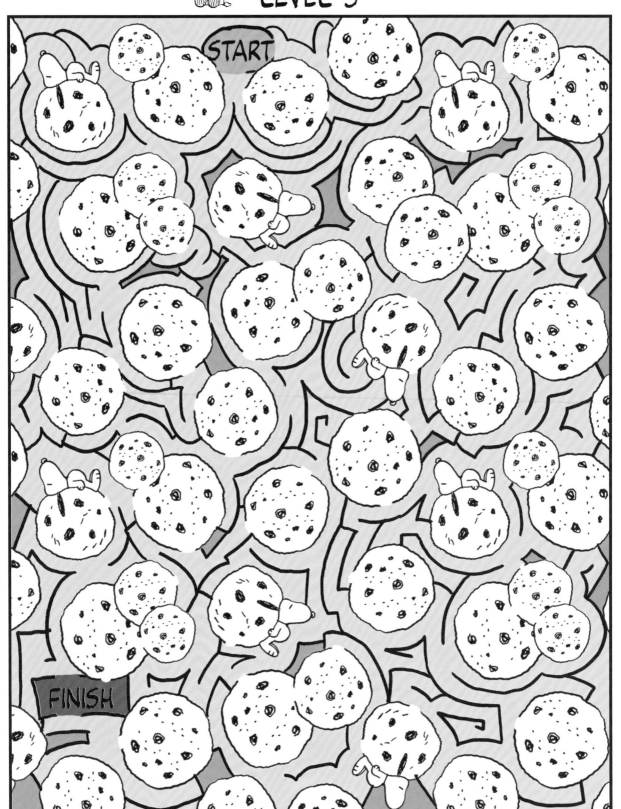

LEVEL 5

LEVEL 5

LEVEL 5

86

LEVEL 5

LEVEL 5

LEVEL 5

LEVEL 5

LEVEL 5

LEVEL 5

LEVEL 5

LEVEL 5

LEVEL 5

LEVEL 5

LEVEL 5

LEVEL 5

LEVEL 5

LEVEL 5

LEVEL 5

SOLUTIONS

1

2

3

4

5

6

7

8

9

10

11

12

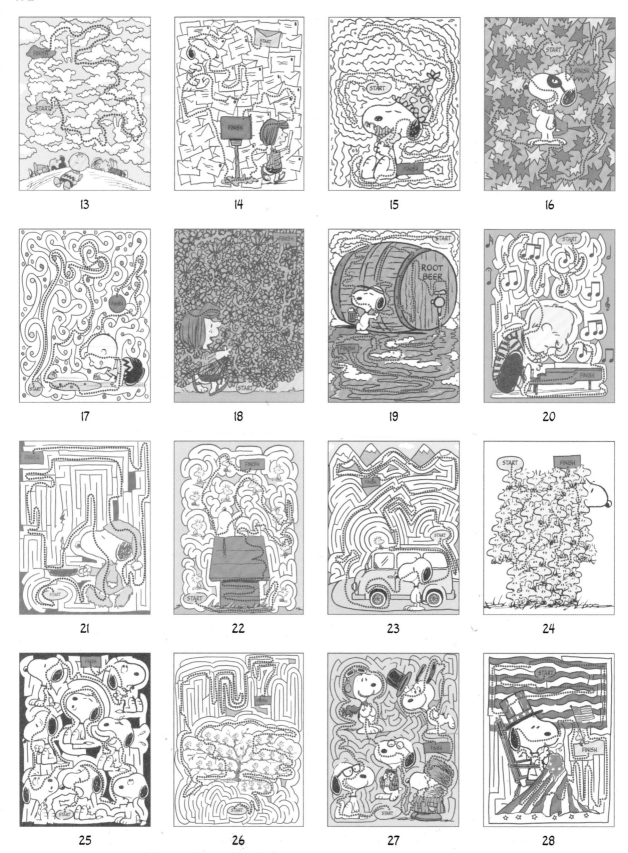

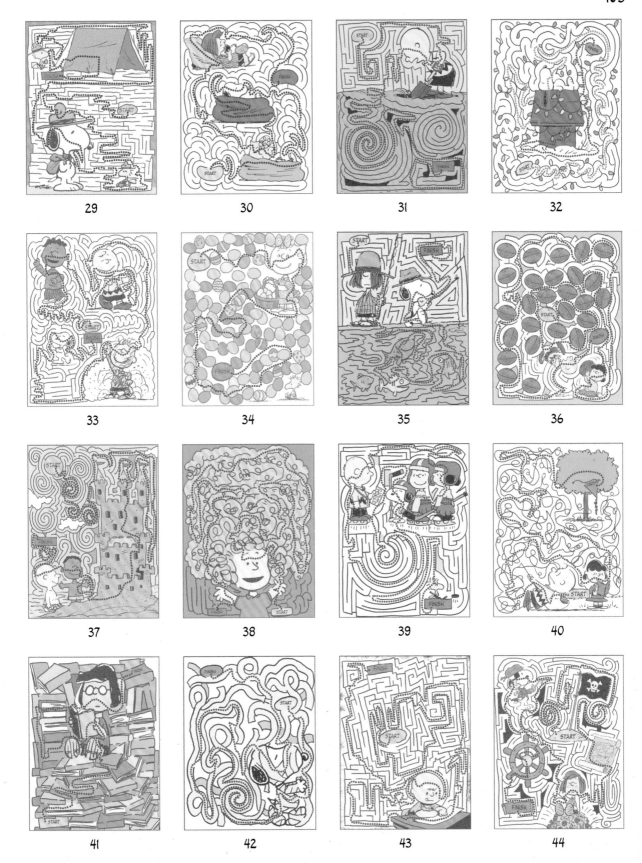

29 30 31 32

33 34 35 36

37 38 39 40

41 42 43 44

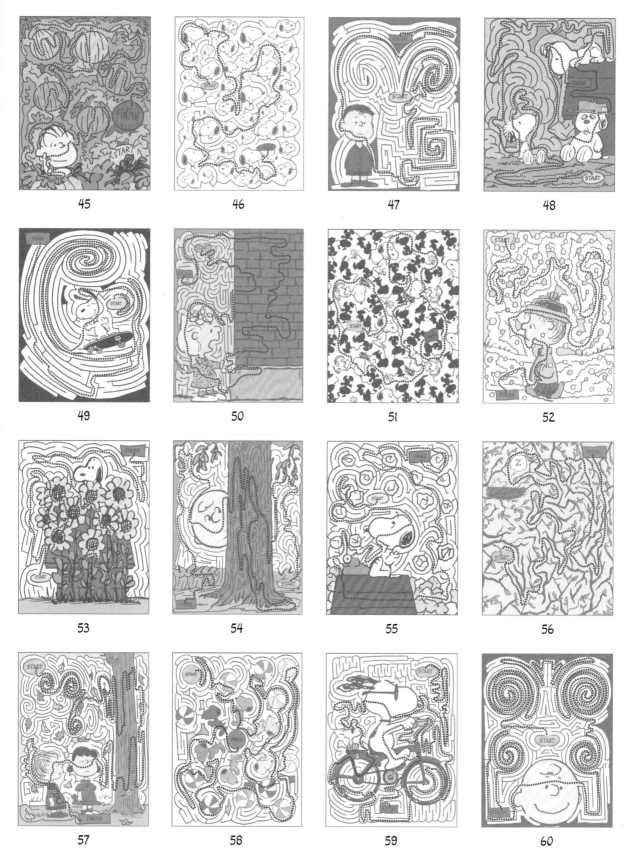

45

46

47

48

49

50

51

52

53

54

55

56

57

58

59

60

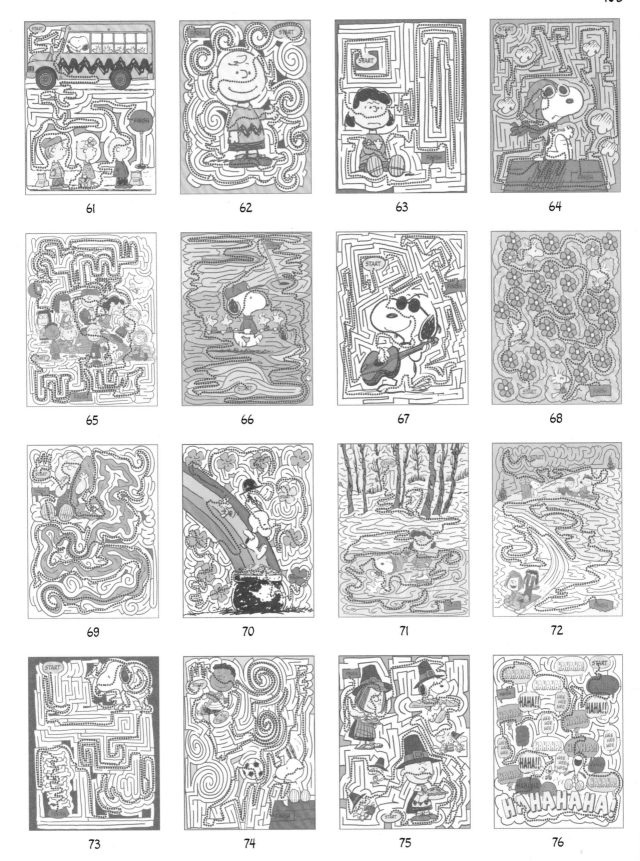

77

78

79

80

81

82

83

84

85

86

87

88

89

90

91

92

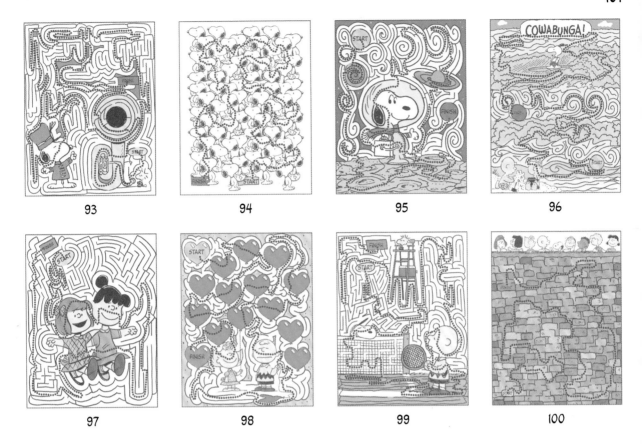

93

94

95

96

97

98

99

100

SPECIAL THANKS TO:

Jean Schulz, Marilyn Allen, Jean Z. Lucas, Craig Herman, Kevin Kotur, Holly Swayne, Alexis Fajardo, Donna Fisher, Andrews McMeel Publishing, Peanuts Worldwide, Creative Associates, Doug Little and the team at Wacom, the National Cartoonists Society, the staff and volunteers of the Charles M. Schulz Museum, and Sparky.

JOE WOS is an internationally recognized cartoonist and master maze maker whose work has appeared in newspapers and books worldwide. He is a recipient of the National Cartoonists Society Reuben Award in the variety category for his unique cartoon illustrated mazes. He established the world record for the largest hand-drawn maze, and his maze murals have been displayed in schools, libraries, and museums. Joe has also had the distinct honor of being the visiting cartoonist of the Charles M. Schulz Museum since its opening in 2002. He has been drawing mazes for over forty years and has heard every variation of the phrase "a-maze-ing!" . . . and he still smiles every time.